To Ian
at Christmas
1990

J.

U.S. NAVY WAR PHOTOGRAPHS

Pearl Harbor to Tokyo Bay

CAPTAIN EDWARD STEICHEN

Standing on an island platform, he studies the surroundings in
preparation for taking one of his outstanding photographs of life on an aircraft carrier.
U. S. Navy Photo

U.S. NAVY WAR PHOTOGRAPHS

Pearl Harbor to Tokyo Bay

Edited by
EDWARD STEICHEN

Text by Tom Maloney

BONANZA BOOKS
NEW YORK

Copyright © 1956, 1980 by T.J. Maloney

All rights reserved.

This 1984 edition is published by Bonanza
Books, distributed by Crown Publishers, Inc.,
by arrangement with Crown Publishers, Inc.,
225 Park Avenue South,
New York, New York 10003

Printed in the United States

Library of Congress Cataloging in Publication
Data

United States. Navy.
  U.S. Navy war photographs.

1. World War, 1939-1945 — Campaigns — Pacific
Ocean — Pictorial works.   2. United States.
Navy — History — World War, 1939-1945 —
Pictorial works.   I. Steichen, Edward, 1879-
1973.   II. Maloney, Tom, 1904-   III. Title.
IV. Title: US Navy war photographs.   V.
Title: United States Navy war photographs.
D767.9.U52   1984   940.54'26   84-16846

ISBN: 0-517-455498

h g f e d c b

PEARL HARBOR—DECEMBER 7, 1941

One of the most remarkable combat photographs
of the war was made at the exact moment
the U. S. destroyer *Shaw* blew up during
the Japanese attack on Pearl Harbor, Hawaii,
December 7, 1941. Photographer unknown, probably
an enlisted combat photographer.

U. S. Navy Photo

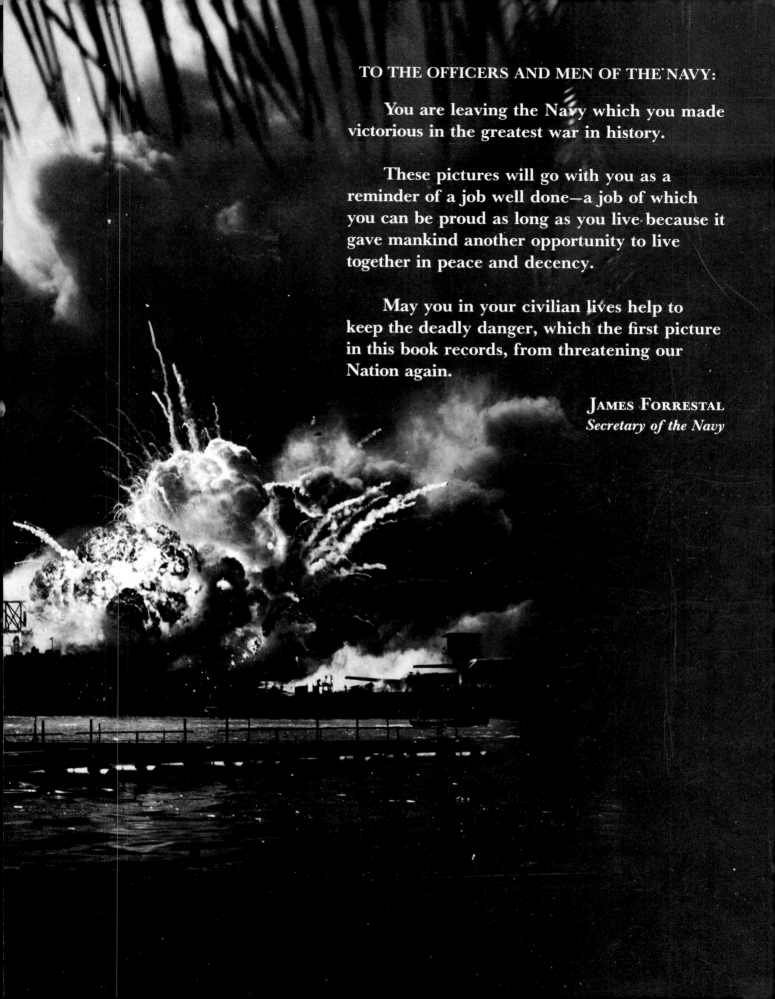

TO THE OFFICERS AND MEN OF THE NAVY:

You are leaving the Navy which you made victorious in the greatest war in history.

These pictures will go with you as a reminder of a job well done—a job of which you can be proud as long as you live because it gave mankind another opportunity to live together in peace and decency.

May you in your civilian lives help to keep the deadly danger, which the first picture in this book records, from threatening our Nation again.

JAMES FORRESTAL
Secretary of the Navy

Foreword

THE HISTORY of *U.S. Navy War Photographs* as a book in this its second edition, thirty-five years after the first, is, I believe, a headliner in the "believe-it-or-not" class.

The first printing in 1945 was 6 million copies. It sold out in less than one year.

Wow! you must be saying. Sounds more like a Navy "Happy-Hour" tall tale than a publishing statement.

But, in truth, the story begins about six months before World War II ended. Secretary Forrestal went to Captain Edward Steichen, the officer in charge of naval photography, with a suggestion for a picture book.

"Can you put together quickly a book of Navy photographs that covers all the Navy actions?"

"Yes."

"Can you get it printed so that it will be available in less than six months?"

"Yes."

"Can you get six million copies?"

"Yes!"

The enormity of the job he had just agreed to rendered Captain Steichen almost speechless. But conditioned by his long association with *U. S. Camera,* the photographic annual, his first query was, "To sell for how much?"

"Nothing. I want to give a copy to every man in the Navy when he returns to his hometown."

Captain Steichen called me and stated: "Secretary Forrestal wants a photo book reviewing the Navy during the war. He wants six million copies. He wants them fast. How fast can we get them?" I didn't know. I was completely flabbergasted. I simply said, "E.J., I don't know. But I'll find out as fast as I can."

Within a very few days I had an answer. My memory may not be exact, but I believe I got three of the largest printers in America to jump aboard and promise to deliver the 6 million copies thirty days after the plates, composition, and paper were ready for their presses.

However, one very important change had to be made in this naval publishing operation. The book planned was oversize, 11″ x 11½″. It was to be a 108-page paperback with a Navy blue and gold cover design. Secretary Forrestal could not find the millions of dollars necessary in his budget to print the millions of copies. The books would have to be sold.

I went back to the printers, hat in hand. The production price that we arrived at was a truly patriotic gesture. Each printer gave me "no-profit" figures, as did the paper companies and engravers: the book was produced for thirty-five cents a copy, and it was sold for thirty-five cents a copy. It sold at a record rate of a million copies a month!

I won't make comparisons, but I think I can state without fear of contradiction that there has never been a publishing endeavor like it in the thirty-five years since the great publishing event occurred. The book has become a collector's item and relatively hard for collectors to find.

So this new edition is now in bookstores and naval stores after a thirty-five-year hiatus. Because it is fondly remembered and Navy men from sea to sea have wondered where they can get this famous Navy book, here it is, with many new photographs, a number of them by Edward Steichen himself.

Edward Steichen was a famous photographer, editor *(U. S. Camera),* horticulturist (president of American Delphinium Society), author *(Family of Man),* and museum director of photography (Museum of Modern Art). He was also always a rather modest exhibitor of his own works and in *U.S. Navy War Photographs* he did not show any of his own photographs. So as one of his closest and dearest friends as well as an ardent admirer, I've taken the liberty of putting six or seven of his own photographs aboard.

Salute! Captain Edward.

TOM MALONEY

Edward Steichen

by Tom Maloney

HE WOULD have been one hundred years old this year; he lived ninety-six of those years. He was born in Luxembourg, grew up in Milwaukee, came to New York in his teens, spent his early 20s in Paris. At twenty-one he took the most famous portrait photograph ever taken in America—of John Pierpont Morgan. He was in charge of photography in the U.S. Army in World War I; U.S. Navy in World War II. He brought modern French art to America and urged Alfred Stieglitz to become its champion. He became the director of photography at the Museum of Modern Art at sixty-eight and remained the active director until his eighty-fifth year. At the museum he produced the "Family of Man," show and book, each of which made photographic history—the book has sold over a million copies.

At the end of World War II he edited the photo book *U.S. Navy War Photographs,* and I helped him sell six million copies in six months, an all-time record.

He loved to discover and aid young people interested in photography. He was affable, handsome, dynamic, sarcastic, and, to me, one of his discoveries, almost infallible. He became my best teacher and the strongest influence in my life.

Although he only finished high school, he was, nevertheless, a superb writer, as his brother-in-law Carl Sandburg was always eager to attest. Thanks to him we produced over twenty-five volumes of *U.S. Camera,* which Carl Sandburg extolled and called the best record of the history of America during the years 1935–1960.

The man of these many accomplishments is Edward Steichen. And his name is as immediate and famous today as it was back in the early 1900s. He needs no further praise, but I want to mention a few of the wonderful things this "boy from Milwaukee" did.

In 1935 I was a young businessman who had just started his own advertising agency. Lejaren Hiller, then a noted photographer, did a series of pictures for me. Hiller was not only a fine photographer, he was also a superb male model. He also grew up in Milwaukee where he and Edward Steichen began their careers in photography. Tom Maloney entered Milwaukee by birth, but about twenty-five years later than these two photo greats.

Thanks to Larry Hiller's photo ingenuity I won a national advertising award for ads using his pictures. My interest in photography sharpened suddenly. I found to my astonishment there was nothing in photo annuals published in the United States to compare with the German *Deutche Lichtbuilt* or the French *Photographie.* I blithely decided there would be and made a so-called dummy, or mock-up, of such a book and went to the most noted photographer in America hoping he'd like the idea and possibly assist me in preparation of the project. Edward Steichen was busy with a picture when I entered his studio. I waited for a half hour until he came to his front office and said, "Young man, what can I do for you?"

"I'd like you to look at this dummy, Mr. Steichen," I said, "and give me your advice and criticism, if you think it worth my getting into a photo book."

He spent fifteen minutes looking at the sample pictures, including one or two of his own. Then he handed it back and said, "These are pretty interesting. Do you think you can get pictures from most of the great photographers in the United States?"

I told him I'd like to try and that Larry Hiller had encouraged me.

"You know Larry?" he asked.

I told him I had worked with Larry and showed him the pictures Larry had done for me.

"Well," he said, "what would you like me to do?"

"I'd like you to edit the book. Choose the pictures you think best for it."

"What!" he said incredulously and added, "By the way, where are you from?"

I played my trump card. "I'm from Milwaukee, Wisconsin."

"You are!" I could feel the warmth in his voice instantly.

"Yes." I replied. "And as you know so is Larry."

"I know. Say hello to Larry for me, and come back and see me in a few days. I want to give this thing some thought, young fellow."

As I remember I didn't have to wait a couple of days. I think it was the next day I received a phone call from him saying he would help me if it didn't take too much of his time. As an old football player I felt as though I had just kicked a world record seventy-five-yard field goal.

The first thing he suggested was a committee to judge the pictures. Every man he mentioned accepted immediately. Never before or since has there been anything like it in photography—Charles Sheeler, Dr. Agha, Arnold Genthe, Anton Bruehl, Paul Outerbridge, Larry Hiller, and Edward Steichen, Chairman.

These were the greatest names in photography: Sheeler, also one of America's foremost painters; Dr.

Agha, a fine photo satirist, and at the time the art director of Condé Nast Publications; Arnold Genthe, famous for his photographs of the San Francisco earthquake; Paul Outerbridge, a great technician, who produced the finest photo color prints in America. Everyone of them respected and admired "E.J.," the number one man in photography and the photo editor of Condé Nast, the publications most noted for great photo usage.

The first issue in 1935 became an instant best seller. It was compared with the German and French annuals and was rated on a par with them. The duo of photo bests became a trio.

Edward Steichen's participation was the major reason for *U.S. Camera*'s dominance. I did the leg work and each year got hundreds of pictures from which he selected those to be used in the annual. Of course the magic of his name made my job relatively simple—every photographer wanted Edward Steichen to see and judge his pictures.

On December 7, 1941, he was spending the weekend with me at my home in Kings Point, Long Island. We were finishing breakfast when the first word of Pearl Harbor came over the air. We listened, stunned, of course, as was everyone. Finally he turned to me, memories of his part in World War I in mind, and said, "I wish I could get into this one, but I'm too old." He was sixty-three.

Within sixty days the Navy was inquiring about the possibility of his taking over and organizing a vast photo effort. Admiral Radford wanted him and publicly proclaimed, "I wouldn't care if he were seventy-three. The Navy wants him and I'm going to get him." He did.

Edward Steichen had many things in his life to be proud of, but I think his Navy title of Captain Edward Steichen, Navy Photography, was the one honor he cherished most. It was, however, far more than an honor. It was a demanding job that would have taxed a much younger man. He was a model of leadership, workmanship, and industry for all of the great young photographers he led in one of the most exciting and important photo assignments ever.

In honor of his one hundreth anniversary, the five thousand contact prints—mostly 3½″ x 4¼″ and 4″ x 5″—which were the cornerstone of his work, go into the archives of the Smithsonian Institution this year. As an Annapolis man myself, I am happy to have been, along with his wife, Joanna Steichen, responsible for this presentation. There have been great photographs in American wars from the Civil War on, but in scope, value, and validity this is far and away the best collection of all.

At the end of the war Edward Steichen was sixty-eight years old. Henry Moe, originator and director of the Guggenheim Foundation and one of the most important directors of the Museum of Modern Art, had become a firm friend of Edward Steichen. One day at luncheon he asked me if I had a suggestion as to who might run the photo division.

"What about Captain Steichen?" I asked.

"I hoped that would be your answer," he said. "Will you ask him?"

By coincidence I was dining with Edward Steichen and Eugene Meyer on Meyer's seventy-fifth birthday.

"E.J.," I said, "Henry Moe has asked me to ask you something."

"What?" he asked.

"Would you accept the position of director of photography at the Museum of Modern Art? Henry wants that."

"Yes. You bet your life I will," he promptly answered. And that began a seventeen-year-career-capping climax to all of Steichen's endeavors. He was sixty-eight when he began and eighty-five when he retired.

He was a great director, and as a memorial to his greatness the museum named its photo area "The Steichen Wing." As always, Edward Steichen immediately put his unique and creative talent to work. He soon embarked on a project that he wanted to be a true expression of the greatness of photography. The end result was an exhibition called "The Family of Man"; most photo enthusiasts and critics consider it the finest photo show ever. While there were other outstanding shows, this was unquestionably his masterpiece. The book of the same title sold in the millions. Steichen donated his royalties to the museum (they have run into the hundreds of thousands of dollars), even though at that time in his life he could have used the money.

Probably the most famous photo portrait ever taken is the picture of J. P. Morgan. Steichen was just twenty-one years old when he took that picture of the financier in 1903. The sitting, which took less than five minutes, is described by Steichen:

I suggested a different position of the hands and a movement of the head. He took the head position, but said, in an irritated tone, that it was uncomfortable, so I suggested he move his head to a position that felt natural. He moved his head several times and ended exactly where it had been "uncomfortable" before, except that this time he took the pose of his own volition. But his expression had sharpened and his body posture became tense, possibly a reflex of his irritation at the suggestion I had made. I saw that a dynamic self-assertion had taken place, whatever its cause, and I quickly made the second exposure, saying, "Thank you, Mr. Morgan," as I took the plate holder out of the camera.

He said, "Is that all?"

"Yes, sir," I answered.

He snorted a reply, "I like you, young man. I think we'll get along first-rate together." Then he clapped his large hat on his massive head, took up his big cigar, and stormed out of the room. Total time, three minutes.

Steichen's friendships were seemingly limitless: Bernard Shaw, Rodin, General Billy Mitchell, Admiral Felix Stump, Eugene Meyer, Condé Nast, Pablo Picasso . . .

As a young man his first devotion was to painting. But as he progressed into photography he became more and more enamored of the lens, less and less of the line. Finally while living in France he decided to concentrate on photography and took all of his paintings, built a bonfire in the yard of his home, and burned them. Yet he did something far more important. He brought the work of the French Impressionists and the French artists of the twentieth century to America. Just a few years ago, on his last trip abroad, Steichen and Picasso got together again for the first time in over fifty years. Both were thrilled to be together again. Picasso, always a funster at heart, needled Steichen. "Edward," he said, "Do you remember when I gave you my first batch of paintings to take back to America and sell?"

"I certainly do," said Steichen.

"Yes," said Picasso, "but you didn't sell any."

"Pablo, you're wrong. I sold three of them. The first three ever sold in America."

Picasso grinned. "Yes, Steichen, you did. I was pulling your leg."

Rodin and Steichen also had a warm friendship and some of Steichen's finest early photographs are of Rodin's sculpture.

I consider Steichen a very great artist and the leading greatest photographer of this time. Before him nothing conclusive had been achieved. I do not know to what degree Steichen interprets, and I do not see any harm whatever, or of what importance it is, what means he uses to achieve his results.

The many, many facets of "E.J." as his friends like to call him could fill a book. I'd like to tell just one more for it was so typical of his easy and intrepid approach to matters large or small.

I was with him when our marines went in to take Iwo Jima. The army and navy were to come ashore within sixty-four hours. "Let's get over to Iwo, Tom, as soon as we can," he said to me.

For two days after we arrived we (or rather he) photographed the island, the action, the Saribochi site, the havoc, the soldiers, the invasion, and its results.

This was a bitter, desolate, godforsaken island. We needed desperately to take it in order to shorten the Guam-Tokyo air trip in case the old B29's ran out of fuel—it was a fifteen-hour nonstop flight and a troubled plane could make it in twelve if we had the airstrip on Iwo. Edward Steichen captured every aspect of it, just as he had captured the essence of J. P. Morgan a half-century earlier.

It was to be his last photo assignment. I have the pictures he took in the few days we were there. In the Pacific as in America and France, the boy from Luxembourg and the man from Milwaukee came through again. His last assignment was as brilliant as his first success.

World War II: Adventures in the Pacific

by Edward Steichen

Most of the world realized too late in the 1930s that Hitler's unchecked progress was leading to another war. All of Hitler's actions—his inflammatory rantings, his humiliating persecution of the Jews followed by his barbaric project for their extermination, his paralyzing invasions of nations after ruthless bombing attacks—all these things piled up and accelerated until finally no one could fail to see that World War II was inevitable.

My own feelings of revulsion toward war had not diminished since 1917. But, in the intervening years, I had gradually come to believe that, if a real image of war could be photographed and presented to the world, it might make a contribution toward ending the specter of war. This idea made me eager to participate in creating a photographic record of World War II. So, early in the autumn of 1941, I went to Washington and tried to interest the Air Force in reactivating my status as a reserve officer. When I arrived, the officer in charge took down my name and address politely, but when he came to the year of my birth, 1879, he put down his pen with an air of finality and told me he was sorry, but I was beyond the age limit for induction into active service.

After this discouraging refusal, I thought my only chance to be of service in photography would be as a civilian. So, as a start, I approached the camera clubs, as I had done early in World War I, with the idea of forming units to photograph the activities of the people and the country. Then David McAlpin, chairman of the Photography Committee and a trustee of the Museum of Modern Art, approached me with the idea of doing an exhibition at the Museum. He assured me that I would have carte blanche. I conceived the idea of doing a contemporary portrait of America, with the title "The Arsenal of Democracy." I had begun collecting pictures for this exhibition when the attack on Pearl Harbor rocked the country. Then, more than ever, I felt my disappointment at not having been readmitted into the Air Force.

While I was in this state of deep discouragement, I received a telephone call from the Navy Department in Washington asking me if I would be interested in photographing for the Navy. I almost crawled through the telephone wire with eagerness. I replied that it so happened I had an appointment in Washington the next day. I took a night train and, at an early hour, turned up at Naval Headquarters. I was heartily welcomed by Commander Arthur Doyle and was introduced to Captain A. W. Radford, who was then in command of training for naval aviators.

When I walked into Radford's office, I saw a look of surprise on his face. He had apparently not been informed that I was no longer a young man. Just then his telephone rang, and while he was talking I was saying to myself, "Boy, you've got to talk fast now." And the moment Captain Radford hung up, I started talking fast, telling him about my service in World War I and stressing my personal experiences under General Mitchell. This seemed to interest him very much, and I followed up quickly with a proposition. I told him I would like to head up a small unit of half a dozen photographers, commissioned by the Navy, to photograph the story of naval aviation during the war. This project interested Captain Radford. He took me to the Assistant Secretary of the Navy for Air to introduce me and to present the idea to him. Again I saw the shocked expression at my age, this time on the Secretary's face. Finally, he said to Captain Radford, "Well, if you really want him, I guess it's all right."

Captain Radford answered, as solemnly as a groom in a marriage ceremony, "I do."

I immediately started assembling a group of young photographers who were very divergent in their work and personalities. It took only a few weeks to select enough men to get the work of the unit organized, but, gradually, we added more photographers. Eventually the unit consisted of Wayne Miller, Charles Kerlee, Fenno Jacobs, Horace Bristol, Victor Jorgensen, Barrett Gallagher, and John Swope, all commissioned in the Navy, and Paul Dorsey, assigned to the unit from the Marine Corps. Navy Lieutenant Willard Mace served as executive assistant. In civilian life, the photographers had worked variously in journalism, documentary photography, illustration, advertising, and marine photography. Off duty, almost every one of them sooner or later came to me separately and said he understood why he had been chosen for the job, but he couldn't understand why some of the others had been.

I soon found that we were a rather irregular unit in the organizational setup of the Navy, and at first we met with opposition from the Navy's regular photographic service. Captain Radford, who soon became Admiral Radford, cleared this away and obtained for our photographers the freedom of movement and action necessary for good photography, but unprecedented in the Navy.

On our first job, we overcame a long-standing navy taboo. Before the war, it was considered undignified for an officer to carry a camera for making official photographs. All this work was assigned to noncommissioned personnel. But at the first naval air station our unit was assigned to photograph, each man turned up with several cameras slung around his shoulders and the usual kit bag of film and accessories. We were all officers, but no one challenged our right to carry a camera, then or at any time during our service.

I sent the men out on missions to various ships, usually aircraft carriers, since naval aviation was our job, and they all turned in exciting pictures. But curiously enough, although each man, in coming into the unit, had expressed enthusiasm for the freedom he would have in doing the kind of photography he wanted, he would invariably come to me before going on an assignment and ask, "Now, just what do you want me to do?"

My answer was always the same. "No one knows just what will happen in war. Photograph everything that happens, and you may find that you have made some historic photographs. But above all, concentrate on the men. The ships and planes will become obsolete, but the men will always be there."

Suddenly, just when naval operations were stepping up, I received a notice that I had reached the Navy's retirement age. Unwilling to retire, I reported this news to Secretary of the Navy James Forrestal, and the next day I was reinstated. But I was listed as disqualified for sea duty. I reported my distress to Admiral Radford, who was about to leave for Pearl Harbor to take charge of naval aviation operations there. He said he would send in a request for my services at Pearl Harbor. That would mean a sea operation was planned and I would go out on sea duty in connection with it. The order came. A junior officer, Victor Jorgensen, and I were to report to Pearl Harbor for temporary duty. When we arrived, we learned that a large navy task force was going to sea the very next morning.

Admiral Radford assigned us to the aircraft carrier *Lexington,* commanded by Captain, later Admiral, Felix Stump. Once at sea, I was informed by Captain Stump that we were going to the Gilbert and Marshall islands to cover the taking of Kwajalein Island by our Marines. I have told this story in full in *The Blue Ghost,* published by Harcourt, Brace and Company. It was illustrated with photographs that Jorgensen and I made on the trip.

Everything about an aircraft carrier is dramatic, but the most spectacular things are the takeoffs and landings of the planes. In all the takeoff pictures I had seen, the planes looked as though they were glued to the deck. They gave no impression of the terrific onrush as the planes

started their run for the takeoff. Nor did they suggest the noise, which is tremendous. Each thundering plane as it takes off emphasizes the contrast between the dynamic intensity of the moment at hand and the dreamlike memories of other places, other times, another life. It makes you aware that it's a cockeyed war in a cockeyed world, in which reality is piling up moments and images as fantastic and incongruous as those dished out by the Surrealists.

There was nothing I could do in the photographs to reproduce the sounds, but I was going to try to give a sense of the motion of the rushing plane. Instead of making a fast exposure to stop the motion and get a sharp picture of the plane taking off, I made a series of exposures around a tenth of a second. One shows a Hellcat fighter plane taking off, its wheels just off the deck. Even the pilot is blurred, while the skipper on the bridge, in the upper left-hand corner, looks on like a benign Zeus.

The long voyage from Pearl Harbor to the Gilbert and Marshall islands was one of the trying things that military personnel always have to deal with: the long, long waiting for what's going to happen, with nothing to do about it. Things changed radically on the day before the Kwajalein Operation. Preparation for the strike brought feverish activity and an atmosphere of tenseness. In the ready room the pilots were being briefed, and on the deck the planes were being armed with bombs. To give an idea of the dramatic impact of the moment, I loaded my camera with infrared film that would darken the blue-gray of the carrier superstructure and the sky.

After the successful Kwajalein Operation, we made a strike on another island. That night we were attacked by a fleet of land-based Japanese bombers and torpedo planes. The attack went on for almost seven hours, aided by bright moonlight and enemy flares which illuminated the entire task force. The *Lexington* was hit in the stern by a torpedo.

This locked our rudder on a sharp turn, and we traveled in circles, making a sitting-duck target; but somehow, we were not hit again. Unfortunately, no photographs were possible, because all lights were doused on the ships. The only way to photograph would have been with flash bulbs, and shooting off flash bulbs would probably have caused us to be dumped overboard by our crew. The *Lexington* was separated from the task force, but the task force commander detailed a cruiser and a couple of destroyers to stay with us while we kept on making great circles. The engineer crew finally managed to straighten out the propeller, but we could not use the rudder.

Steered only by the propeller, we made slow progress away from the scene of action.

I assumed that a ship struck by a torpedo would sink, so I tried to prepare a kit consisting of a dry camera and a supply of film placed inside an aerograph balloon. Jorgensen and I had planned this emergency procedure and had practiced inserting the camera in the balloon. With the two of us working, it was very easy. But working alone, all I could do was stretch open the balloon in one direction. Not having a third hand, I was not able to open it wide enough to drop in the camera, which I held ready in my teeth.

I was on the bridge at the time. Captain Stump came along and asked me what I was doing. I told him I was trying to get my camera into the balloon so that I would have a dry camera when we abandoned ship. At this, the captain and the rest of the officers on the bridge burst into laughter. Unwittingly, I had served the purpose of breaking the tension. Captain Stump assured me we would remain afloat and there would be no call to abandon ship.

We limped back to Pearl Harbor, where temporary repairs were made, and then proceeded to the United States for the complete reconditioning of the ship.

I made another trip into the Pacific to Guam and Iwo Jima. I arrived in Iwo Jima the day after it was declared secure. That night, a number of fliers who had arrived the same day were killed by Japanese soldiers who came out from hiding places underground and dropped hand grenades into the tents of the sleeping men. Earlier that day I had made the picture of a dead Japanese soldier, buried except for the fingertips either in a shell explosion or by a bulldozer.

Shortly after this, Secretary Forrestal signed an order placing me in direct command of all navy combat photography.

Steichen on Photography

PHOTOGRAPHY HAS become an indispensable tool in nearly all fields of human activity. As a witness of places, times, and events, it records with an exactness beyond the scope of any other visual means. Because of the magnitude and variety of these functions, its esthetic potentialities are sometimes overlooked. When practiced by the artist, photography becomes a medium capable of giving form to ideas and incisive expression to emotions.

The photographer is served by a technique differing completely from that practiced by the painter, who begins with blank surface and then by more or less complicated procedures, always under complete control, is able to achieve a growth and realization of his concept. The photographer begins with a completed image; and compared with the painter, the controls available to him are hardly worth the mention. By the same token there are no primitive or archaic phases in photography. The process itself was born as a completed achievement and most of the earliest photography suffers little by comparison with that of today.

The Museum of Modern Art was the first museum to make the art of photography an important part of its program. It is unique among art museums in the extent of its recognition of photography. While the museum possesses outstanding examples of some of the earliest photography, its collection is predominantly of twentieth-century prints. It contains the work of widely recognized photographers as well as experimental and exploratory work by newer talents—work marking a continuing effort to penetrate the surface appearance of reality or seeking to translate into pattern and design the magic details of a fragment of growth or of deterioration.

In the collection there are prints that give evidence of man's passionate search for truth, rendered with technical precision and mental precision, separately or on occasion together. The swift freezing of an exact instant; the gamut of feeling written on the human face in its contrasts of joy, serenity or despair; the beauty of the earth that man has inherited and the wealth and the confusion that man has created within this inheritance—all these are rendered with a sense of timelessness and exactitude. The art of photography as it is used on the printed page or in exhibitions, as well as in films and television, is moving swiftly toward wider and wider horizons.

Today's photography ranges from a meticulously precise naturalism to the completely abstract image; from the searching electron micrograph in the field of science to images expressing a highly sensitized emotional concept; the frozen action made possible by speed-lights in contrast to the blurred action of slow exposure or of superimposed images.

It is the artist in photography who beyond his own creative achievement establishes new standards, influences, and uses of the medium, whether it be in the service of science, education, or communication.

There is a new kind of aliveness in the melting pot of American photography. This aliveness is not based on novelty, slickness, or on any particular kind of technical skill or procedure. There are fine warm accents and sharp emphasis on the mirroring of human relations, and there is a boisterous gaiety, sly humor, and whimsicality as well as bitter or ironic comment. There is the aloofness of icy objectivity and the challenge of various approaches in the rendering of meaningful abstractions, and there is grace and wit in concrete elements of design and the magic of an exact instant.

Some of the work is still tentative and some consciously or unconsciously repetitions of much that has gone before. Along with photographs expressing the fulfillment of mature experience, we also find heartening encouragement in the restless seekings, probing aspirations and experiments of younger photographers.

Good photography in any field becomes alive by virtue of the quality and integrity of the photographer's perception and feeling. When the photographer's emotional reaction is carried through the over-all organization of the image and under the control of an informed intelligence, the resulting photograph takes on the incandescence of truth. The casual candid snapshot of people on the street, bus, or subway can be as dead, senseless, or "corny" as any sentimental silhouette against a sunset sky.

The photographer who is primarily interested in finding definitive approval for his favorite cult, cant, or ism, or some affirmation about the limitations of the medium is apt to find that modern photography is puzzling and contradictory, for our best photographers are attracted to the medium because it is young, elastic, and has elbowroom to grow in—lots of elbowroom!

EDITOR'S NOTE: The above quotations are excerpts from prefaces to various exhibitions directed by Edward Steichen for the Museum of Modern Art and appear here through the courtesy of Mr. Steichen and the museum.

PEARL HARBOR–DECEMBER 7, 1941

PEARL HARBOR–DECEMBER 7, 1941

ADM. NIMITZ

Adm. Nimitz was the Navy chief in the Pacific actions, headquartered in Guam. A shrewd tactician, he was also a very popular director of operations. He is revered as one of the great officers to serve in the U.S. Navy. Photographed by Capt. Edward Steichen, USNR. U. S. Navy Photo

**OFF DUTY IN CREW'S QUARTERS ON THE AIRCRAFT
CARRIER *YORKTOWN***

Letter-writing, letter-reading, and just plain loafing, these crew members
of an aircraft carrier relax during off-duty hours. The ship is operating in
tropical waters and the men are stripped down against the heat.
Photographed by Sp(P)1/c Alfonso M. Iannelli, USNR. U. S. Navy Photo

THE FIGHTING LADY

Aerial view shows the USS *Yorktown* landing her planes. Most of the
footage for the motion picture *The Fighting Lady* was shot on the USS
Yorktown. Photographed by Lt. Comdr. Charles Kerlee, USNR.
U. S. Navy Photo

CAMERA SHUTTER STOPS SIXTEEN-INCH PROJECTILES
FROM THE BATTLESHIP *MISSOURI*

One of our Navy's mighty Iowa-class battleships, the *Missouri,* is shown as
her sixteen-inch guns fire in salvo from the forward turret. At the upper
right six projectiles are shown in flight. Photographed by Sp(P)2/c Arthur
T. Statham, USNR. U. S. Navy Photo

23

THE USS *TOLMAN*—DESTROYERS ARE PROUDLY AND AFFECTIONATELY DUBBED "CANS"

During Okinawa operations, destroyers acting as radar pickets took the most vicious attacks any ships endured. In one morning two destroyers were hit by twelve Kamikazes, shot down thirteen more, and yet managed to survive. U. S. Navy Photo

ECHELON OF GRUMMAN AVENGERS

These powerful bombers carry a crew of three. Included in their armament is a belly tunnel gun, visible beneath the insignia on the fuselage. Avenger flyers and the torpedoes they launched with deadly accuracy scored many important successes against units of the Japanese fleet. Photographed by Lt. Comdr. Horace Bristol. USNR.
U. S. Navy Photo

PBM IN JET-ASSISTED TAKEOFF

A massive twin-engined PBM takes off, assisted by a jet that enables this
heavy Navy plane to shoot up from the water like a Fourth of July
skyrocket. Photographed by Lt. Comdr. Horace Bristol, USNR.
U. S. Navy Photo

HANGAR DECK OF THE USS *YORKTOWN*

Ordnance men arming planes on the hangar deck of the USS *Yorktown*,
while in the background men off duty are watching a movie.
Photographed by Lt. Comdr. Charles Kerlee, USNR. U. S. Navy Photo

MURDERER'S ROW—SIX GREAT CARRIERS IN ULITHI ANCHORAGE

Read from foreground to background: USS *Wasp*, USS *Yorktown*, USS *Hornet*, USS *Hancock*, USS *Ticonderoga*, and USS *Lexington*, anchored at Ulithi before a strike on Japan. U. S. Navy Photo

CONVOY IN A STORM OFF HVALFJARDI, ICELAND
"In the Navy you get every snootful of the sea there is." U. S. Navy Photo

**MUNITIONS EXPLODE ON A U. S. CARGO SHIP
FOLLOWING HITS BY NAZI DIVE BOMBERS–SICILIAN
INVASION**

A photographer caught this picture from the deck of a Coast Guard–
manned combat transport. Fire started by bombs dropped amidships
spread rapidly to the ship's munitions supply, which exploded to make
this a dangerous though picturesque scene. Photographed by Warrant
Officer W. J. Forsythe, USCGR. U. S. Coast Guard Photo

**THE OLD USS _LEXINGTON_ ORDERS "ABANDON SHIP"—
CORAL SEA, MAY 1942**

The destroyer alongside is taking off the sick and wounded while the able-
bodied are sliding down ropes and being picked up by small boats. Not a
man was lost in abandoning the ship. U. S. Navy Photo

31

THE *ENTERPRISE* IN ACTION—BATTLE OF SANTA CRUZ, OCTOBER 26, 1942

A Japanese bomb splashes astern of the U. S. carrier as the enemy plane pulls out of its dive directly above the carrier. Another enemy plane is pictured (center) after making an unsuccessful dive on the carrier. A flash of the battleship's batteries may be observed, and a destroyer can be seen astern of the battleship. The cruiser from which this picture was taken leaves a curving white wake as she turns rapidly. The *Enterprise*, known in the fleet as the "Big E," established a proud fighting record during the war. Photographed by CPhoM Lauren Frazer Smith, USNR. U. S. Navy Photo

JAPANESE BOMB HITS FLIGHT DECK OF USS
ENTERPRISE—AUGUST 24, 1942

The film from his camera was saved, but this unique and famous picture
cost the photographer his life. Photographed by PhoM3/c Robert
Frederick Read, USNR. U. S. Navy Photo

TAKEOFF FROM CARRIER *LEXINGTON* FOR DEFENSE OF TARAWA

Photographed by Capt. Edward Steichen, USNR. U. S. Navy Photo

JAPANESE HEAVY CRUISER KNOCKED OUT BY CARRIER PLANES—BATTLE OF MIDWAY, JUNE 1942

A Japanese heavy cruiser of the Magami class lies dead in the water after having been bombed by U. S. carrier-based naval aircraft. Photographed by a USS *Enterprise* photographer. U. S. Navy Photo

**TARAWA—MARINES IN FRONTAL ASSAULT TAKE HEAVILY
REINFORCED PILLBOX**

At the order to charge, Marines swarmed over pillbox on Tarawa, braving
fire from all sides. The only way to silence the suicidal pillbox defenders
was for the Marines to fight to the top and shoot down inside at the
Japanese. Photographed by Warrant Officer Obie Newcomb, Jr., USMCR.
U. S. Marine Corps Photo

**THE MARINES INCH FORWARD AGAINST SUICIDAL
RESISTANCE ON PELELIU ISLAND**

The leathernecks battled stiff resistance on this "Gibraltar of the Rising
Sun," in the Palau Group of the Caroline Islands. Photographed by Pfc.
John P. Smith, USMCR. U. S. Marine Corps Photo

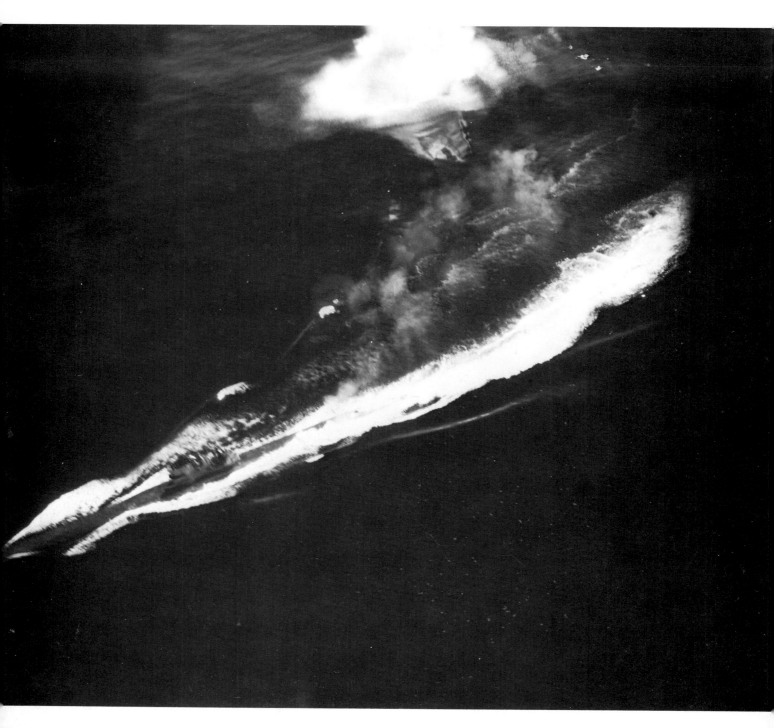

**SURFACED NAZI SUBMARINE UNDER ATTACK BY ESCORT
CARRIER PLANES—ATLANTIC CONVOY LANES**

Shepherding a convoy, our planes carried the fight to Nazi "wolf packs."
Seeking out the subs as they began to converge, Escort Carrier *Bogue*
dispersed the undersea foe with such stunning blows that no sub came
within miles of the convoy. Photographed by a USS *Bogue* photographer.
U. S. Navy Photo

**ESCORT CARRIER PLANES CIRCLE THE LARGE SLICK
WHERE NAZI SUB SANK**

Serpentine wake marks the sub's path to the circular oil slick where she
sank. Photographed by CPhoM A. W. McEleny, USNR. U. S. Navy Photo

**ESCORT CARRIER PLANES DROP ASH CANS ON NAZI
SUBMARINE**

The escort carriers ended the growing German submarine menace.
Submarine crew members crouch near conning tower as another ash can
heads toward them. U. S. Navy Photo

**FIVE-INCH GUNS FIRE DURING A NIGHT ATTACK—
SOLOMONS, OCTOBER 21, 1943**

Photographed by PhoM1/c Glenn E. Reed, USNR. U. S. Navy Photo

THE COAST GUARD CUTTER *SPENCER* ON ATLANTIC
CONVOY DUTY DEPTH CHARGES AND DESTROYS A NAZI SUB

Coast Guardsmen on the deck of the cutter *Spencer* watch the explosion of
a depth charge which blasted a Nazi U-boat's hope of breaking into the
center of a large convoy. The depth charge tossed from the 327-foot cutter
blew the submarine to the surface, where it was engaged. Photographed
by Warrant Photographer Jess W. January, USCGR. U. S. Coast Guard Photo

INVASION SUPPLIES—EVERYTHING BUT THE KITCHEN SINK

The Navy in addition to its battle responsibilities became a vast transport
operation ably assisted by the Coast Guard. While tonnage figures are
unavailable, they were probably into the billions. Photographed by
PhoM1/c Don C. Hansen, USCGR. U. S. Coast Guard Photo

**BLASTING GUAM SHORE DEFENSES PREPARATORY
TO INVASION — July 20, 1944**
U.S. Navy Photo

**LCI'S UNLOAD TROOPS ON RED BEACH AT MOROTAI
ISLAND—SEPTEMBER 1944**

Landing troops on island after island in the Pacific was not a new
maneuver, but the Navy developed more efficient techniques and
effectively overpowered Japanese resistance at sea as well as on shore.
Photographed by a USS *Santa Fe* photographer. U. S. Navy Photo

**THE UNITED STATES MARINES LAND AT CAPE
GLOUCESTER**

Carrying their rifles high, Marines wade through a three-foot surf at Cape
Gloucester from their LST and immediately assemble at designated spots
to push into the New Britain jungle and lay siege to the Japanese-held
airport. Photographed by Sgt. Robert M. Howard, USMCR.
U. S. Marine Corps Photo

INVASION OF CAPE GLOUCESTER—MARINES AND COAST GUARDSMEN PREPARE A CAUSEWAY FOR LANDING

This photograph became one of the most popular invasion pictures. It appeared in millions of copies of magazines and newspapers.
Photographed by CPhoM Edward Schertzer, USCGR.
U. S. Coast Guard Photo

**SAND BAGS FOR GUN EMPLACEMENTS ON A BEACH AT
LEYTE, P. I.**

Veterans of several amphibious invasions along the long road from the
Solomons to the Philippines, LST's unload their men and machines on the
beach of Leyte. Photographed by PhoM1/c James C. W. Munde, USCGR.
U. S. Coast Guard Photo

**LST HIT BY JAPANESE BOMBER—"HERE COMES
ANOTHER"**

As the rescue boat approaches the burning LST, all hands prepare for
another attack from Japanese bombers. Photographed by Y3/c Daniel B.
Murphy, USNR. U. S. Navy Photo

**THE USS *PENNSYLVANIA* BLASTS GUAM SHORE DEFENSES
PREPARATORY TO INVASION—JULY 20, 1944**

Invasion of Guam meant the capture of an island that would become a
major base for the planned invasion of Japan. The Navy and the Air
Corps began important offensives to the Japanese mainland from Guam as
soon as the island was secured. Photographed by a USS *Chenango*
photographer. U. S. Navy Photo

51

FOURTEEN-INCH GUNS BOMBARD GUAM—JULY 1944

U. S. Navy Photo

**THE AMPHIBIOUS ASSAULT ON IWO JIMA—
FEBRUARY 19, 1945**

Marines in landing craft hit the beach at Iwo Jima on February 19, 1945.
At the left center is Mt. Suribachi, nicknamed "Hot Rock" by the Marines
who took the island. This aerial photograph was flown to Guam,
transmitted by radio, and was printed in an American newspaper within
fifteen hours after it was made. U. S. Navy Photo

**THE BEACH AT IWO JIMA, D-DAY—A WAVE OF U.S.
MARINES BEGINS ATTACK**

A wave of Fourth Divison Marines begins the attack, as another boatload
of battle-tested veterans is landed on the beach by assault craft.
Photographed by T/Sgt. H. Neil Gillespie, USMCR. U. S. Marine Corps Photo

**U. S. MARINES HIT THE BEACH ON IWO JIMA—
FEBRUARY 19, 1945**

While smoke and dust from the fight on the slopes of Mt. Suribachi blur
the outline of the volcano, U. S. Marines that afternoon hit the beach
where the first waves landed in the morning. Photographed by Pvt. Bob
Campbell, USMCR. U. S. Marine Corps Photo

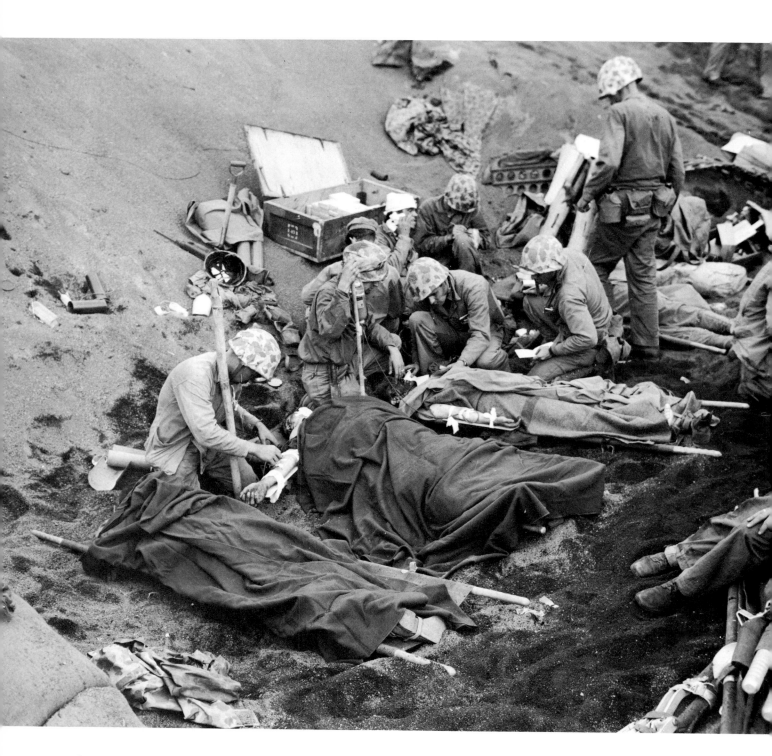

**BLOOD PLASMA AND WHOLE BLOOD—NAVY DOCTORS
AND CORPSMEN TREAT MARINES ON IWO JIMA**

Some of the most heroic moments of the war were valiant attempts by
naval doctors and corpsmen to save lives of the wounded and to do
everything possible to relieve the anguish of all who needed assistance.
Photographed by Warrant Officer Obie Newcomb, Jr., USMCR.
U. S. Marine Corps Photo

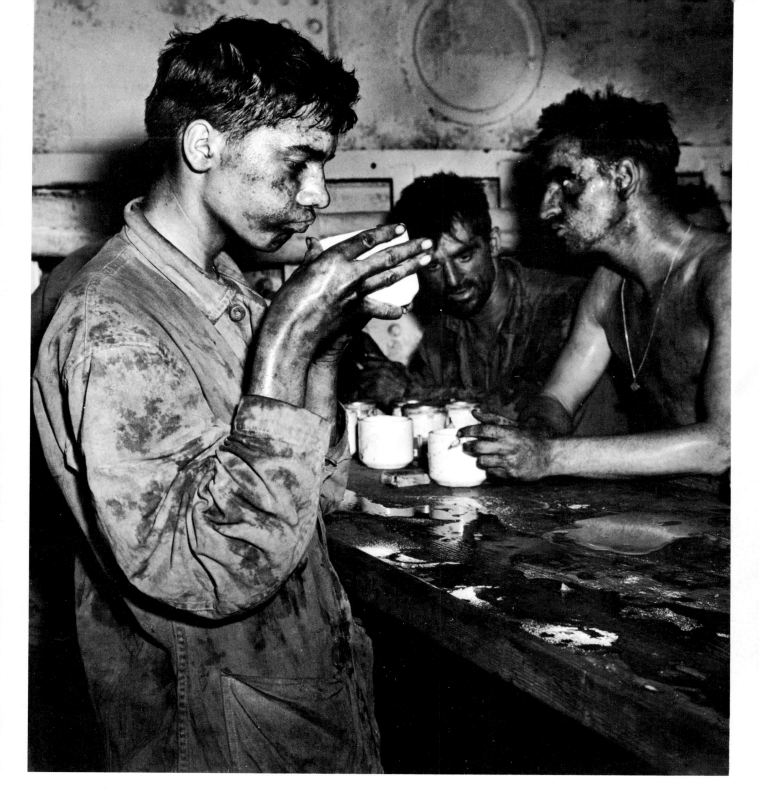

**COFFEE FOR THE EXHAUSTED CONQUERORS OF ENGEBI
ISLAND–THE UNITED STATES MARINES**

This picture was also very popular with the American press. The trio
expressed perfectly the total mental and physical fatigue that follows in
the wake of battle. Photographed by CPhoM Ray R. Platnick, USCGR.
U. S. Coast Guard Photo

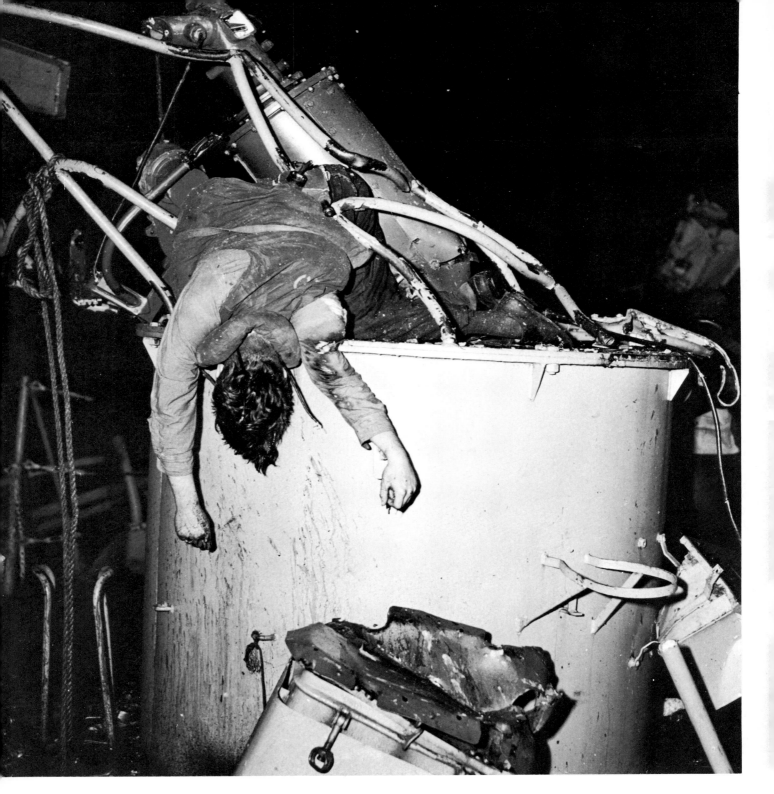

HIS BATTLE STATION

The atmosphere of death and of the futility and senselessness of war is
graphically portrayed here. Photographed by PhoM1/c Arthur Green, USCGR.
U. S. Coast Guard Photo

**CREW BUNKS WITH THE TORPEDOES ABOARD A
U. S. SUBMARINE**

Our submarines had a most impressive record in all oceanic areas East and
West. Total tonnage sunk was our surest indication of how close we were to
victory. Japanese and German shipping were virtually eliminated before
peace was declared. Photographed by Lt. Comdr. Charles Fenno Jacobs, USNR.
U. S. Navy Photo

**TORPEDOED JAPANESE DESTROYER PHOTOGRAPHED
THROUGH PERISCOPE OF THE U. S. SUBMARINE *WAHU***

This remarkable photograph, the first combat action photograph taken
through the periscope of an American submarine, shows an enemy
destroyer after it had been struck by two torpedoes launched by the
submarine from which the picture was taken. The destroyer sank in nine
minutes. Rising Sun insignia appears on top of the turret to the left. Two
men in white scramble over the conning tower to the right. U. S.
submarines sank over 5 million tons of enemy shipping. U. S. Navy Photo

**DAWN ATTACK BY DOUGLAS DAUNTLESS DIVE
BOMBERS—WAKE ISLAND BURNS BELOW—DECEMBER 1943**
Another widely reproduced Pacific combat shot. The photographer
Charles Kerlee was a noted West Coast commercial
photographer before joining Capt. Ed Steichen's naval unit.
Photographed by Lt. Comdr. Charles Kerlee, USNR. U. S. Navy Photo

63

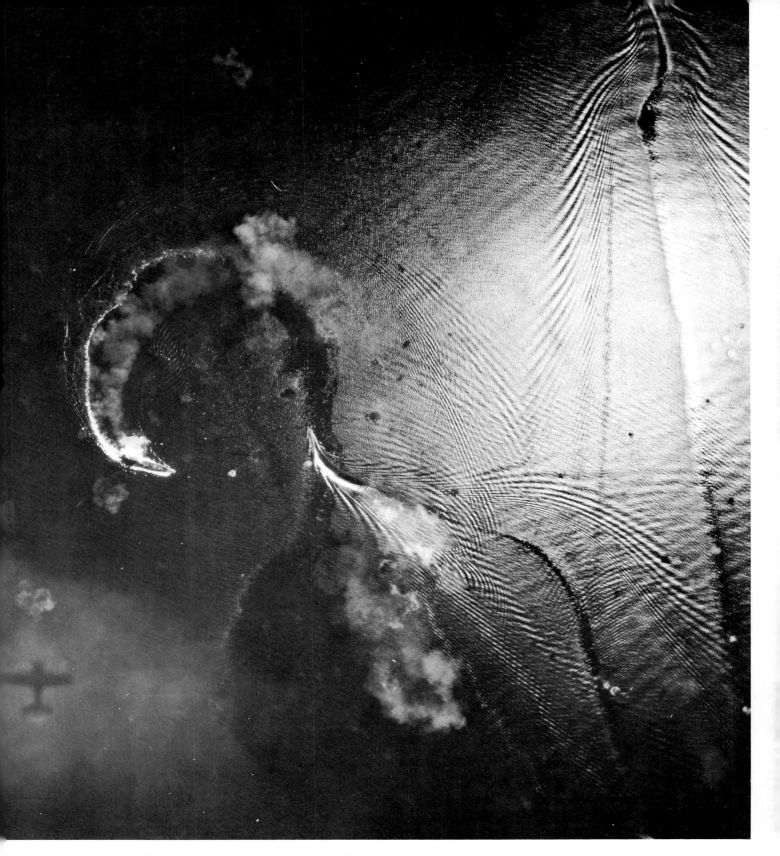

DIAGRAM OF DOOM FOR JAPANESE FLEET—SECOND BATTLE OF THE PHILIPPINE SEA

The wake of a fleeing Japanese ship etches a gigantic question mark in the waters of Tablas Strait as it vainly dodges the aerial attack of Navy planes from Admiral Halsey's Third Fleet and Vice Admiral Kinkaid's Seventh Fleet in the Second Battle of the Philippine Sea. The wakes of other Japanese ships can be seen as well as the shadow of one of the Navy attacking planes. In this action, approximately sixty enemy ships were sunk. Photographed by an aircrewman. U. S. Navy Photo

**CARRIER HELLDIVERS SCORE DIRECT HITS ON TWO
JAPANESE TRANSPORTS SOUTH OF LUZON—
NOVEMBER 25, 1944**

Photographed by an aircrewman. U. S. Navy Photo

**HELLDIVERS RETURNING FROM GUAM STRIKE—
JULY 1944**

Guam was the first U. S. possession retaken from the Japanese.
Photographed by PhoM1/c O. L. Smith, USNR. U. S. Navy Photo

**JAPANESE FLEET UNDER ATTACK BY CARRIER-BASED
AIRCRAFT WEST OF MARIANAS—JUNE 19, 1944**

A large Japanese carrier, Shokaku class, burning from bomb hits, turns
sharply to starboard while damaging near-misses land off her bow and
stern. Photographed by an aircrewman. U. S. Navy Photo

JAPANESE CARRIER BOMBED AND TORPEDOED BY NAVY PLANES—OCTOBER 24, 1944

Her flight deck buckled by a torpedo explosion and punctured by bombs from Navy dive bombers, this Zuiho-class Japanese carrier maneuvers violently to escape further blows. She sank the same day. Photographed by an aircrewman. U. S. Navy Photo

SCRATCH ANOTHER MEATBALL—SAIPAN OPERATIONS

Navy photographers were brilliantly adept at catching enemy planes and ships as they were hit by American missiles and shells. Photographed by a USS *Kitkum Bay* photographer. U. S. Navy Photo

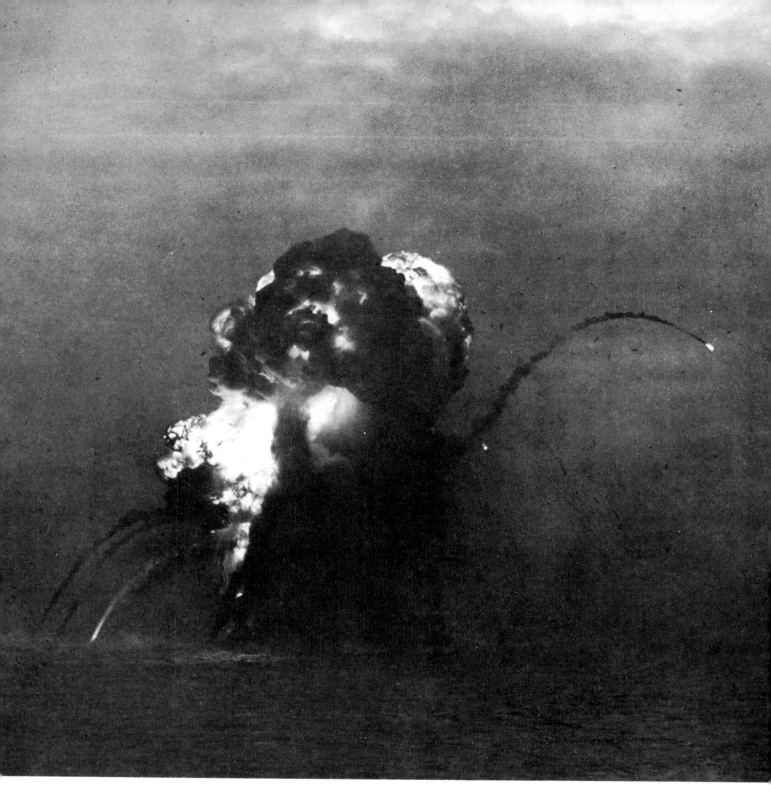

COUP DE GRACE FOR THE FATALLY WOUNDED USS
PRINCETON—OCTOBER 24, 1944

The huge geyser of smoke and flame marks the death of the light carrier
USS *Princeton* as it is hit by our torpedoes after all hands abandoned ship.
The *Princeton* was damaged during a Japanese air attack in "round one"
of the Second Battle of the Philippine Sea. Desperate efforts were exerted
to save the ship, but flames and internal explosions defeated all hopes of
salvage. U. S. Navy Photo

**ESCORT CARRIER TAKES A BEATING FROM ENEMY
FLEET—PHILIPPINE SEA, OCTOBER 25, 1944**

The USS *Gambier Bay* is bracketed by shells from the Japanese Fleet that
the Seventh Fleet carrier escort group fought off in the Second Battle of
the Philippine Sea. Photographed by a USS *Kitkum Bay* photographer.
U. S. Navy Photo

**CARRIER PLANES DESTROY JAPANESE CONVOY OFF
FRENCH INDOCHINA—JANUARY 12, 1945**

U. S. Navy Photo

**AIRCREWMAN WOUNDED IN STRIKE ON RABAUL—
AIRCRAFT CARRIER USS *SARATOGA*, NOVEMBER 5, 1943**
Photographed by Lt. Wayne Miller, USNR. U. S. Navy Photo

**AIRCREWMEN IN READY ROOM PREPARE GRIMLY FOR
ANOTHER STRIKE—NOVEMBER 5, 1944**

Veteran aircrewmen put on flight gear for a strike against Manila. Sober
faces show they know what they are up against. Photographed by Lt.
Wayne Miller, USNR. U. S. Navy Photo

THE 40MM GUNNERS KNOCKED JAPANESE KAMIKAZES FROM THE SKY

Photographed by Lt. Comdr. Charles Kerlee, USNR. U. S. Navy Photo

**GUNNERS OF THE USS *HORNET* SCORE A DIRECT HIT ON
JAPANESE BOMBER—MARCH 18, 1945**

Photographed by a USS *Hornet* photographer. U. S. Navy Photo

JAPANESE SUICIDE PLUNGE THAT MISSED AND CRASHED ALONGSIDE THE USS *SANGAMON*

U. S. Navy Photo

**DIRECT HIT—*YORKTOWN* GUNNERS DESTROY JAPANESE
TORPEDO PLANE OFF KWAJALEIN, DECEMBER 4, 1943**
Photographed by CPhoM Alfred Norman Cooperman, USNR.
U. S. Navy Photo

**CLOSE-UP OF JAPANESE KAMIKAZE JUST BEFORE HE
CRASHED ON USS *ESSEX*—NOVEMBER 25, 1944**
Photographed by Lt. Comdr. Earl Colgrove, USNR. U. S. Navy Photo

**A KAMIKAZE CRASHES ON FLIGHT DECK OF THE *ESSEX*,
FORWARD OF NUMBER 2 ELEVATOR**

Photographed by a USS *Ticonderoga* photographer. U. S. Navy Photo

PLANES OVERHEAD–THEIRS OR OURS? MINDORO INVASION

Antiaircraft gun crews of a U. S. Navy cruiser strain to spot the status of an unidentified plane overhead. U. S. Navy Photo

**GUNNERS ON THE USS *YORKTOWN* WATCH TWO
KAMIKAZE DIVE BOMBERS ATTACK THE USS *INTREPID***

One plane crashes aboard the *Intrepid*'s deck while its bomb explodes
beside the carrier; the other plane misses the carrier and crashes near the
bomb splash. Photographed by PhoM1/c William Helms, USNR.
U. S. Navy Photo

THE USS *BUNKER HILL* TAKES TWO KAMIKAZES IN THIRTY SECONDS—MAY 11, 1945

While operating with a fast carrier task force in the "slot" between Okinawa and Kyushu, these two suicide hits, acting as fuses to the gasoline-filled and bomb-laden planes, set the stage for one of the most heroic battles of the Pacific. Fighting suffocating flame and exploding rockets and bombs, the gallant crew, her heroes unnumbered, sacrificed 392 dead or missing and 264 wounded to save their ship. Photographed by a USS *Bunker Hill* photographer. U.S. Navy Photo

**THE *BUNKER HILL* PHOTOGRAPHED A FEW SECONDS
LATER FROM ANOTHER SHIP**
Photographed by a USS *Bataan* photographer. U.S. Navy Photo

EXPLOSION FOLLOWING HIT ON THE USS *FRANKLIN* BY JAPANESE DIVE BOMBER—MARCH 19, 1945

Operating less than sixty miles from the Japanese coast, with many of her planes fully armed and fueled, the carrier was suddenly attacked by an enemy dive bomber, which scored hits with two 500-pound armor-piercing bombs. Gutted by flame, listing badly and suffering more than a thousand casualties, the carrier limped the thousands of miles back to New York. Photographed by a USS *Santa Fe* photographer. U. S. Navy Photo

JAPANESE FREIGHTER PEPPERED BY CARRIER-BASED PLANES—JALUIT ATOL, FEBRUARY 16, 1944
Dramatic strafing attacks off the Marshalls produced these geysers around the ship and set it afire. U. S. Navy Photo

CREW ESCAPES AS NAVY PLANE GETS "DUNKING"

Crashing where its wing tip hit the water on a sharp backing turn, a Navy
Avenger involuntarily got "the deep six" as those aboard escaped unhurt.
U. S. Navy Photo

**RELIGIOUS SERVICES UNDER THE BLASTED FLIGHT
DECK OF THE USS *FRANKLIN***

Chaplains were a highly respected group of people in the Navy. They
often served as gunnersmate and always served as morale builders and
friends. Photographed by CPhoM R. Woodward, USNR.
U. S. Navy Photo

**JAPANESE SUICIDE PLANE ATTACK ON THE BATTLESHIP
USS *MISSOURI***

The desperation tactics of Japanese suicide planes were only occasionally
successful. Gunfire from U.S. ships was not only accurate but deadly in
most cases, before the suicide plane came near enough to crash on board.
In this picture the doomed plane was very nearly successful in landing and
exploding. Photographed by a USS *Missouri* photographer. U. S. Navy Photo

**IMPACT AND EXPLOSION OF JAPANESE PLANE ON FLIGHT
DECK OF THE *INTREPID*—NOVEMBER 25, 1944**

Four times the USS *Intrepid* was battered into flames by Japanese air
action, and four times the big Essex-class carrier returned to fight again.
Photographed by a USS *Intrepid* photographer. U. S. Navy Photo

**BATTLING FIRES ON THE CARRIER *INTREPID*
FOLLOWING KAMIKAZE CRASH**
Photographed by Lt. Barrett Gallagher, USNR. U. S. Navy Photo

JAPANESE SUICIDE PLANES HIT THE USS *TICONDEROGA*
OFF FORMOSA—JANUARY 21, 1945

Smoke pours from a bomb hole in the deck of the USS *Ticonderoga*, where the first of two Japanese suicide planes crashed into her while she was operating off the coast of Formosa. The second suicide plane crashed near the Number 1 elevator. The thick cloud of black smoke in the top right-hand corner comes from the elevator. U. S. Navy Photo

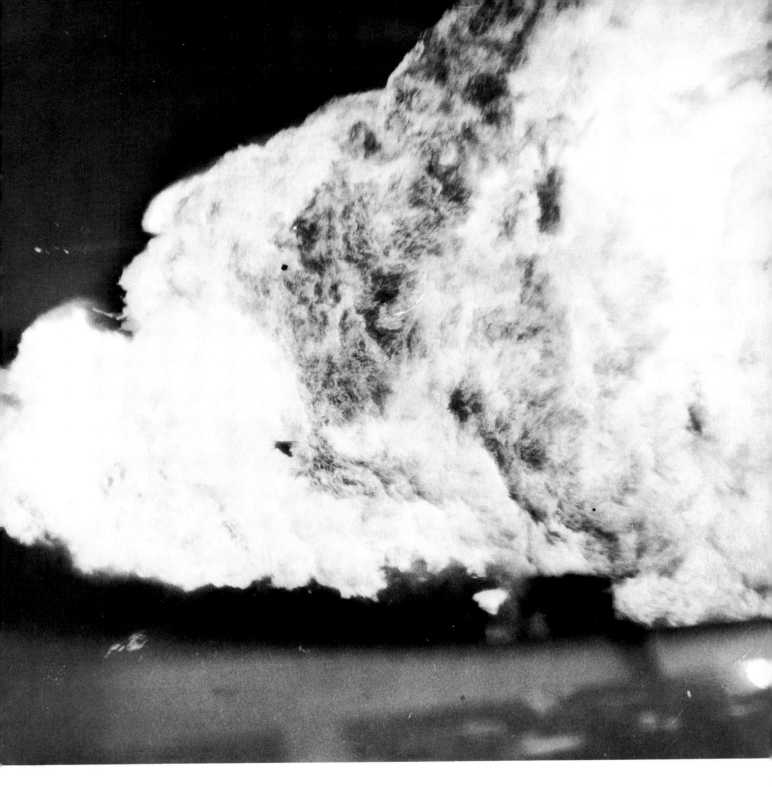

**JAPANESE BOMBER CROSSES DECK IN FLAMES—MISSES
THE USS *LUNGA POINT* BY INCHES**

Photographed by a USS *Lunga Point* photographer. U. S. Navy Photo

93

**TRANSFER OF WOUNDED FROM THE USS *BUNKER HILL*
TO THE USS *WILKES BARRE***

Sick bays aboard carriers and battleships were actually medium-sized
hospitals. U. S. Navy Photo

HELPING HAND OF THE COAST GUARD
The hand is reaching out from the rail to swing a wounded Marine
aboard. Photographed by CPhoM Ray R. Platnick, USCGR.
U. S. Coast Guard Photo

SEABEES AT HOLY SERVICES—SANDBAG SEATS IN A CANVAS CHAPEL

The Seabees became the pride of the Navy. Most of them were, for one reason or another, ineligible for the draft, but their record in construction, reconstruction, or any situation that required engineering assistance was so remarkable that they were accorded the highest respect. They were particularly effective in both the installation of facilities on invasion and the expansion of these facilities the moment an island was secured. Photographed by Chief Carpenter's Mate H. F. Merterns, Fiftieth Seabees. Official Seabee Photo

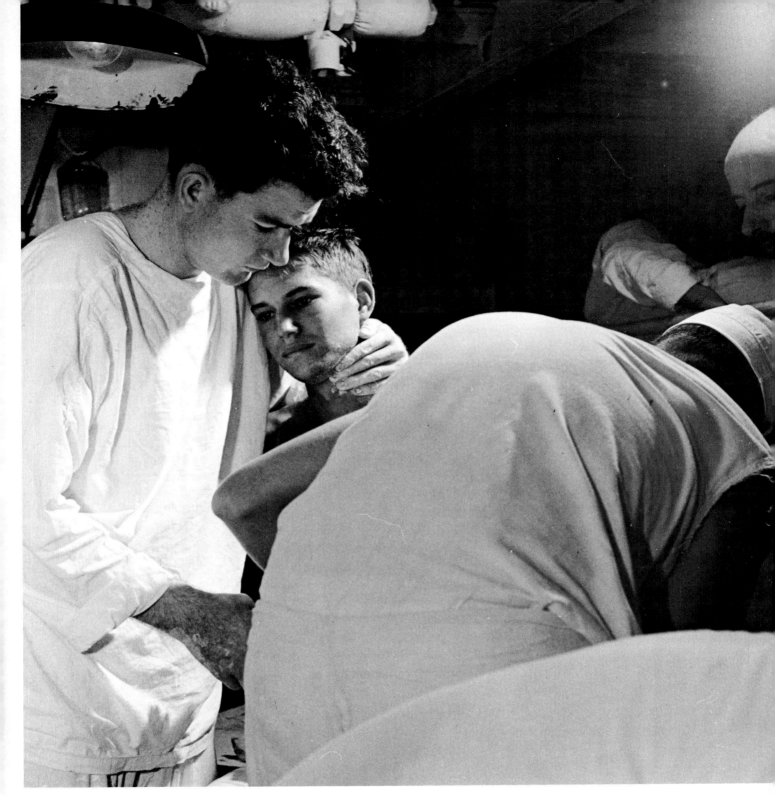

**DOCTORS AND CORPSMEN TREAT OKINAWA CASUALTIES
ON HOSPITAL SHIP *SOLACE*—MAY 1945**

Casualties on landings, especially early in the Pacific invasion days, could
be very heavy. This picture of a seemingly underaged sailor is not atypical.
But it is an unusually fine photograph by another of Capt. Steichen's
famous Navy crew. Photographed by Lt. Victor Jorgenson, USNR.
U. S. Navy Photo

**THE SEABEES DID A PAUL BUNYAN IN THE PACIFIC—BUILT
HARBORS AND MOVED ISLANDS**
Photographed by Lt. Comdr. Charles Fenno Jacobs, USNR.
U. S. Navy Photo

**WARRIOR IN TRUNKS—NAVY UNDERWATER DEMOLITION
TEAMS BLASTED INVASION CHANNELS TO THE BEACHES**
Carrying out some of the most dangerous and difficult assignments of the
war, members of these teams, unarmed and garbed only in swimming
trunks, swam to action, braving enemy fire to destroy with explosives any
natural and man-made obstacles on the beaches. U. S. Navy Photo

FIRST BATTLE OF THE PHILIPPINE SEA

Lt. (j.g.) Alexander Vraciu, USNR, of Chicago, Illinois, signifies he shot down six Japanese in this battle, June 1944. U. S. Navy Photo

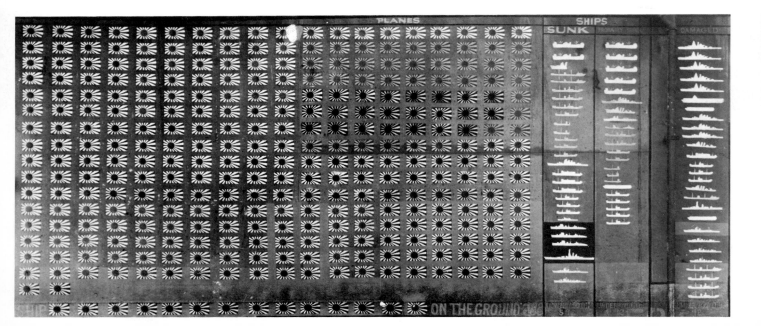

REAR ADM. FELIX STRUMP

The skipper relaxing aboard his carrier after successfully repulsing a Japanese attack. Photographed by Capt. Edward Steichen, USNR. U. S. Navy Photo

SCOREBOARD OF THE USS *INTREPID*

In 15 months of combat operations the *Intrepid*'s guns and planes sank 80 ships and destroyed 650 aircraft. U.S. Navy Photo

**AMTRACKS MOVE IN AS BATTLESHIP FIRES SALVOS—
OKINAWA, APRIL 1, 1945**

Photographed by Lt. Gil DeWitt, USNR. U. S. Navy Photo

LSM'S (R) SEND VOLLEYS OF ROCKETS TO THE SHORES OF TOKASHIKI SHIMA—MARCH 1945

U. S. Navy Photo

MARINE CORSAIR CUTS LOOSE WITH EIGHT 5-INCH ROCKETS OVER OKINAWA

Photographed by Lt. David Duncan, USMCR. U. S. Marine Corps Photo

MARINES SMOKE OUT JAPANESE FROM A CAVE AT NAHA, OKINAWA
Photographed by Sgt. Thomas D. Barnett, Jr., USMCR.
U. S. Marine Corps Photo

TIRED MARINE AND DOG SLEEP ON A BED OF ROCKS— OKINAWA
Photographed by Pfc. R. G. West, USMCR. U. S. Marine Corps Photo

LEATHERNECKS AND A NATIVE BOY SHARE FOXHOLE ON OKINAWA
Photographed by Sgt. William McBride, USMCR. U. S. Marine Corps Photo

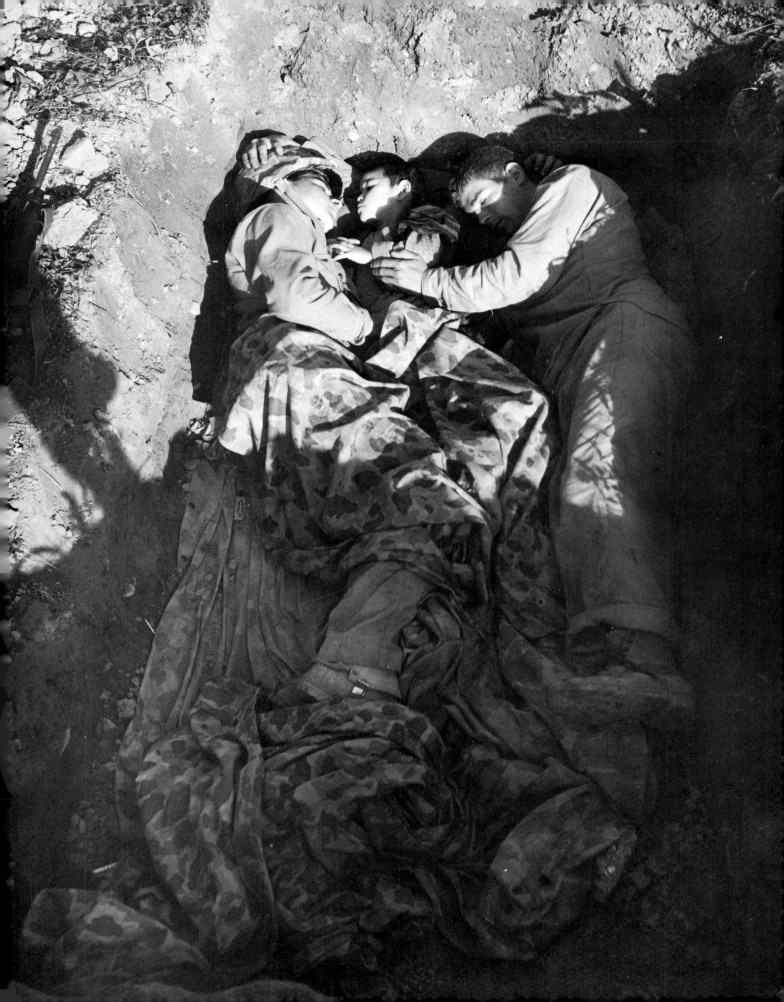

TORPEDO BOMBERS ARE BRIEFED FOR STRIKE
Crew lines up while ship and planes are readied for strike on Kwajalein.
Photographed by Capt. Edward Steichen, USNR. U. S. Navy Photo

CARRIER-BASED PLANES PLASTER THE BATTLESHIP
HARUNA—KURE AREA, JULY 28, 1945

This is an exceptionally good shot of the devastation bombers could do to any ship the enemy had in combat areas. Planes were particularly effective against battleships and carriers because the size of these ships made them better and easier targets. The success of our own air combat efforts is testified to by the fact that we lost more heavy ships in Pearl Harbor than we did during the whole of the war in the Pacific. U. S. Navy Photo

**SWEATING IT OUT—LISTENING IN ON CARRIER
INTERCOM TO BOMBERS OVER TINIAN, JULY 11, 1944**

A loud speaker brings voices of bomber pilots talking to each other, over
the interplane phone system. This interplane talk is picked up by the
carrier's radio and transmitted through the loud speaker in the pilots'
ready room. Photographed by Lt. Victor Jorgenson, USNR. U. S. Navy Photo

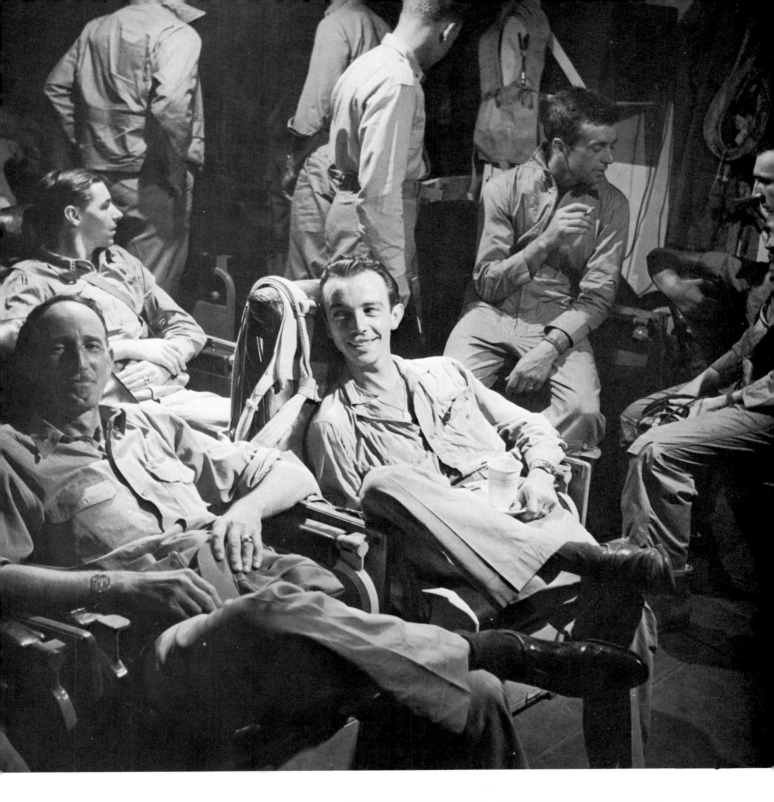

MISSION COMPLETED — ALL BOMBERS RETURNING
Photographed by Lt. Victor Jorgenson, USNR.
U.S. Navy Photo

TWO OF THE NAVY'S MOST FAMOUS FIGHTER PILOTS
Lt. Comdr. E. H. O'Hare, USN *(left)* and Lt. Comdr. J. S. Thach, USN.
U. S. Navy Photo

HILARIOUS WELCOME
Vice Adm. John S. McCain, USN, being greeted by Capt. Harold M.
Martin as he steps off his plane. U. S. Navy Photo

THE BATTLESHIP *YAMATO* SUNK BY NAVY PLANES—EAST CHINA SEA, APRIL 7, 1945

The largest and mightiest Japanese battleship blows up just before
sinking. Eight bomb and eight torpedo hits were made by Navy pilots.
Besides the *Yamato,* Fast Carrier Task Force planes sank two cruisers and
three destroyers on the same day. U. S. Navy Photo

HELLCAT ROARS OFF FLIGHT DECK OF "THE BLUE GHOST"—THE USS *LEXINGTON*

This photo taken aboard the USS *Lexington* was one of Capt. Steichen's own. He had a special feeling for takeoff shots, contrasting action with a still background. Photographed by Capt. Edward Steichen.
U. S. Navy Photo

**STRIKE ON TOKYO—FIFTY-TWO CARRIER-BASED PLANES
PASS MT. FUJIYAMA, FEBRUARY 1945**

Photographed by Comdr. G. A. Heap, USN. U. S. Navy Photo

**VIEW OF MT. FUJIYAMA THROUGH THE PERISCOPE OF A
U.S. NAVY SUBMARINE**

Periscope pictures were rather few and far between because of the
difficulties involved in taking them. This unusual shot rather dimly
captures Japan's most famous mountain, located sixty-five miles south –
west of Tokyo. U. S. Navy Photo

117

**THE THIRD FLEET MANEUVERS OFF THE COAST OF
JAPAN—AUGUST 17, 1945**

Photographed by Lt. Barrett Gallagher, USNR. U. S. Navy Photo

HOMEWARD BOUND

The colors wave jauntily as the fleet returns after another successful engagement. Photographed by Comdr. Horace Bristol, USNR.

U. S. Navy Photo

GRAVE OF AN UNKNOWN U. S. MARINE ON SAIPAN

Lt. Paul Dorsey USMC was a famed photographer long before he re-entered the Marine Corps at an advanced age. He was highly respected both personally and for his ability by the young photographers in Steichen's naval unit. Photographed by Lt. Paul Dorsey, USMCR. U. S. Marine Corps Photo

**TO THE DEAD ARE ACCORDED THE HONORS THAT GO
ONLY TO HEROIC MEN OF THE SEA WHO DIE IN BATTLE—
BURIAL AT SEA WITH FULL RITE AND RITUAL WHILE
THEIR SHIPMATES, WITH ALL THE DIGNITY OF THE
LIVING, PAY SILENT TRIBUTE**

Photographed by a USS *Lexington* photographer. U. S. Navy Photo

NEWS OF DEFEAT COMES TO JAPANESE PRISONERS OF WAR—GUAM

News of the defeat and unconditional surrender of Japan reached these Japanese prisoners of war at a POW camp on Guam, when with bowed heads they heard Emperor Hirohito broadcast to the people of Japan. U. S. Navy Photo

ALLIED PRISONERS CHEER VICTORY—AOMORI NEAR YOKOHAMA

Waving the flags of the United States, Great Britain, and Holland, Allied prisoners of war at Aomori wildly cheer approaching units of the fleet, August 29, 1945. U. S. Navy Photo

**SUNSET OVER FUJIYAMA–U. S. FLEET IN TOKYO BAY,
AUGUST 29, 1945**

Mt. Fujiyama, as symbolic of Japan as are Tokyo and the Islands, well
deserves its romantic background. Everyone in the American Navy hoped
to see Fuji, preferably aboard ship. As this picture shows, many indeed
did. U. S. Navy Photo

TOKYO HARBOR—SEPTEMBER 2, 1945

The signing of the surrender aboard the *Missouri* was one of the most
momentus events in American history. Pictured here are Adm. Nimitz, at
the moment of signing, and *(left to right)* Gen. Douglas MacArthur, Adm.
William Halsey, and Rear Adm. Forrest Sherman surrounded by our
contingent of officers on the *Missouri*. U. S. Navy Photo

A NAVY FLYER'S CREED

I am a United States Navy flyer.

My countrymen built the best airplane in the world and entrusted it to me. They trained me to fly it. I will use it to the absolute limit of my power.

With my fellow pilots, air crews, and deck crews, my plane and I will do anything necessary to carry out our tremendous responsibilities. I will always remember we are part of an unbeatable combat team—the United States Navy.

When the going is fast and rough, I will not falter. I will be uncompromising in every blow I strike. I will be humble in victory.

I am a United States Navy flyer. I have dedicated myself to my country, with its many millions of all races, colors, and creeds. They and their way of life are worthy of my greatest protective effort.

I ask the help of God in making that effort great enough.

U. S. Navy Photo